Bill's Wanderings and Diaries

by

William James McKay

Printed and bound in Vancouver, B.C. Canada
by Standard Press

Acknowledgment

The cover of this book was done by my great uncle Len Whalen, whose cartoons appeared in the Hiballer Forest Magazine for twenty years, and in the Vancouver Sun. His father Bill Whalen with his four brothers founded the pioneer Whalen Pulp and Paper Co. in Howe Sound area. Len spent most of his life in Vancouver and White Rock, British Columbia.

Dedication

This book is dedicated to my mother, who has been an inspiration in my life, and my best friend.

A Picnic in the Woods

One June morning, several years ago, my mother suggested what she thought would be a fun trip. My mother, 2 brothers and myself packed a few things and went to our cottage. Her idea of fun was to pack a lunch and head off to a piece of property that she planned to build on and cut some trees down. While mother sat in the middle of the lot drawing plans for her dream house, she pointed out trees that should be cut.

We had lots of fun that day and my brother really knew how to fell those trees. After cutting up the wood, my brother thought we should try and sell it. We stacked up two chords and put a "Wood for Sale" sign on it; in no time we had sold all the wood. It was a fun trip.

A couple of months later a friend of mother's wanted to take her for a drive, so she suggested going by the lot to show him what a great job her son's had done. To her dismay she realized that she had cut trees down on her next door neighbours lot!

Nov 20th, 1984

I had saved some money and decided to take a bus

trip to Port Townsend, Washington. I was living on my own and I thought the trip out of town would be good for me. That night of Nov 20th, I arrived in Port Townsend and stayed in a hotel next to a bar overlooking the ocean. A fellow was celebrating his 34th birthday in the bar when I arrived to have a beer. It was a tranquil night of celebrating. The next day I took a tour of the town, looking at the old homes, some of which had a bed & breakfast. The layout of the town reminded me of an old western movie with charming old homes overlooking the ocean. That night I took the bus back to Vancouver. It was an enjoyable trip.

Nov 20, 1985

On this day, I took a trip to Victoria, B.C., I was hoping to surprise a friend I had not seen in awhile. I had in the past been to his house, and therefore I thought I could locate it. I remember getting off the bus and walking about a mile in blizzard conditions to his home. Night fall had settled in as I attempted to walk up the hill. With the wind against me and the snow blowing hard, I was certainly not prepared for the worse. I was wearing black oxford shoes which were very slippery, and having a very bad time trying to climb this hill. When I finally made it to the top, I was freezing cold and felt like I was going to die. I remembered the street name my friend had lived on, and I asked this young lady if I was headed in the right direction. She said yes and pointed the street out to me. Walking down this street I recognized his house. Knocking at his door, a couple answered and told me he and his family had moved a couple of years before. Being related to my friend they gave me his stepmother's telephone number. (Later I found out from her that he had moved to Edmonton.) That evening I had found my way back to downtown Victoria and stayed in a hotel for the night. Reminiscing back, I settled into bed and watched some television. I heard these eerie noises as if someone was whispering to me. I would turn the volume down on the television and hear silence, then I would turn it up and hear whispering again. This went on for half an hour and it made me feel very uneasy. Later I had found out it was the wind blowing through the crack in the front door. After knowing that, I slept well that night. The next morning I watched the Donahue show. It was about Alaska men living in a small town, looking for wives.

(Mail order brides.) It was interesting. Later that night, I arrived back safely in Vancouver on the Greyhound bus.

March 1, 1986 Box Car Willie

On this particular night, I tried riding a freight train from Bellingham to Mount Vernon, Washington but was unsuccessful. So instead, I took the Greyhound bus around 8:00 PM and arrived in Mount Vernon at 8:45 PM. I had previously found a telephone number in a Bellingham newspaper for work on a farm in Mount Vernon. But unfortunately, the job had been filled. Knowing then the job had been filled, I decided that I would try and hop a freight train to Spokane. Finding where the freight yard was I waited for the train. A couple of trains did pass in the right direction, but did not stop and were traveling too fast to jump on. My hopes had faded away, and I was getting cold, tired and hungry. I did not have enough money for a hotel. After wandering around town and seeing the sights, I was getting tired. I found my bed for the night under a fir tree. There were grass clippings under the tree and this made a nice mattress for me except the grass gave off a terrible odor. I was sleeping on a vacant lot with houses on either side of me. The only means of keeping warm was to put my long johns on, which I had taken along with me at the time. Surprisingly, I was quite warm throughout the night and I woke up only a couple of times. I had just enough money in my pocket the next morning to get back to Bellingham and that is what I did. I had a good friend in Bellingham that let me stay at his house the next few days. It was a box car dream that failed, but I gave it a good try, and I am satisfied with the end result.

June 1, 1987 Dangerous Chance
Around 4 PM I went to Buck's tavern in Bellingham, Wash. to have a few beer. I was enjoying myself, dancing the night away and did not leave until 2 AM. I was feeling rather drunk and decided to hitchhike home. I did not even have a jacket on. Anyway, these two young fellas picked me up and I rode in the back of their pickup. They drove like mad men trying to throw me out the back by swerving and jamming the brakes on. We passed two policemen on the way and that is when I should have jumped out of the truck but I didn't and then they dropped down to a

deserted beach area. Luckily a train crossed the crossing so they had to stop and that's when I decided to jump out. I was so mad at both of them and let them know, and that's when I got spat in the face by the passenger of the truck. I got scared and ran up behind some apartments. By this time I thought they had turned around and left. So I decided to go back out on to the road and walk home. As I entered the road, to my surprise, they came driving around the corner with their lights out trying to run me down, so I dove for cover in some prickle bushes. I got back up stumbling and they then tried running me over in reverse gear. Again, luckily they just missed me. By this time, they had blocked my only route to safety with their vehicle. Determined, I ran past them in a drunken daze, up behind some apartments, and into the front of one, banging hard on the glass door which scared them off. (They both did chase me but I did not look around to see if they were carrying any weapons.) After banging on this door, I waited about 5 minutes but nobody did answer. When I thought the coast was clear, I slowly made my move up to the road, and there is where I saw my enemy drive off in the opposite direction with their lights off.

Dec 10, 1988

Today I went over to Salt Spring Island for my first time. I spent a couple of quiet days in a motel reading my bible. When I returned to Vancouver, I went to live with my grandmother for awhile. My uncle who is a Jesuit priest from Oregon U.S.A., came up for Christmas to visit his mother (my grandmother). It was nice to see my uncle for Christmas.

Jan 24, 1989

I went over to Tofino on the west side of Vancouver Island for a few days. The purpose of my trip was to help out with an oil spill. On Jan. 28, when I returned to my grandmother's house in Vancouver, my relatives were celebrating my uncle's birthday (the Jesuit priest). We all had a great time.

April 1, 1989

This was the first day of a month's agony with a toothache. I could not have the work done on my tooth until May 1, 1989 because they were booked up until that time. By the end of May, after having a root canal done, my tooth felt much better.

July 10, 1989
On this day I went with a friend in his car to
Helena, Montana, U.S.A. He was going on a
business trip and he asked me if I would like to go
along with him on the ride. I stayed for a few days,
then I took the Greyhound bus back to Vancouver.
My friend stayed on in Helena.

July 18, 1989
Starting on this day I did some roofing work for a
friend and finished on July 23, 1989. On the night
of July 25, I phoned my sister for her birthday.

August 28, 1989
My mother has a summer cottage near
Bellingham, Wash. on the Mt. Baker Hwy. I stayed
here for three weeks, went outside everyday and
enjoyed my surroundings. There are beautiful
mountains, streams and trails to explore. It was an
enjoyable vacation.

Sept 26, 1989
My younger brother is a truck driver. Today at
5 AM we transported a truck load of lumber over
to Port Alberni. We brought back another load of

lumber from a sawmill in Port Alberni, and we got delayed at the weigh station for 2^1/$_2$ hours. The reason is because my brother's load was 5,000 pounds over weight. We arrived back into Vancouver at 10:00 PM.

Sept 29, 1989
Arrived at the Fraser River at 5:15 PM. It is an old section of Marpole, a suburb of Vancouver. I frequently like to wander there. At 6:30 PM, I crossed paths with my native friend named Laylan. I followed him up the hill to a heritage site where, according to him, natives had been buried for one thousand years. The smell of fall, the sun going down behind the autumn leaves, and Laylan's presence all made me feel as carefree as a child again. A happy peaceful feeling came upon me as I frolicked and explored new territory that my friend had pointed out to me. At 8:00 PM we built a fire by the river and talked about many things, which included my friend's first recollection of the Fraser River when he was growing up (Laylan is 20 years my senior). He was the first person to start a trail through what is now called the Fraser Angus Lands. Talking with Laylan around the fire

that night, I felt the strong presence of the elders all around us. They were there in the crashing of waves washing up against the shoreline, the wind that howled, and most importantly the elders were around the beaver we saw that night. From where we sat quietly at the river's edge, you could almost reach out and touch the beaver. It sensed that we would not harm it. We put our fire out around 12 AM, and went our separate ways. I rode the bus and arrived back home at 12:30 AM.

Oct 8, 1989 Walking in the Woods

It's a beautiful, sunny day and I hear frogs, planes, and distant human voices. When it is really quiet you can hear the leaves falling. A father with his two children ride past me on the windy trail. I sense he is a warm and affectionate father. There's silence again, an aroma of crisp clean air, nature's way of showing her love, and solitude to the happy wanderer. The beat of a different drummer approaches me on his bicycle. He is in his own little world with no time for his fellow man, or even the sounds of nature around him. All he hears is the thumping of his heart beat in time with his bicycle gears. The stranger rides off, I probably will never have that encounter again in this life. With the moment to myself, I enjoy nature to it's fullest. Listening, watching the sun peek through the trees and down upon a spider, who appears to be sleeping in his web. I close my eyes and remember when I was child. It seemed that the days had been long, with no responsibility, fun with lots of good times.

Oct 9, 1989 The End of My Day

Passing noisy skateboard, distant sound of lawnmower, young girl sitting outside her home talking on her cellular phone, sound of footsteps approaching from behind me, an early smell of discharged firecrackers, squealing bike brakes, breathing in the autumn air, standing on top of a hill, appreciating every precious moment, the far off, luscious, green mountains with dangling white clouds all around. Strolling by a nearby park, under huge trees, with soft peachy color leaves, a small boy repeatedly strikes his soccer ball up against the wall of a building. And that was the end of a wonderful day.

Nov 13, 1989

I left the house at 2:00 PM today, and it was starting to rain lightly. I decided to go back into the house and put my rubber boots on. When I went back outside, a couple of old friends pulled up in a car. I had had a disagreement with one of these friends not too long ago. Still feeling uneasy about being around him, I told him I would call him after supper. They both then left and I went to visit my church as I had planned earlier. Upon arriving at church, I felt a strong desire to pray about the situation with my friend. There was nobody else present during my stay, and the silence was very uplifting for my mind and soul. After my visit at the church, I went for a walk through some nearby woods. The air was fresh with the rain falling lightly and the color of the leaves was breathtaking. After supper I did call my good friend, and we sorted out a lot of different things. We are both back on good terms with each other. That night I went to sleep with a clear conscience.

Nov 14, 1989

Another day has arrived, and it is already 9:00 AM.

Last night when I put my head down on my pillow, I went out like a light. A good night's rest was the result of clear conscience. After washing my face, I knelt for 30 minutes on my bedroom floor reading my breviary. Next on the agenda, I put some warm clothes on. Having some toast, coffee and porridge, gave me the energy I needed for the morning. Walking in the woods, nearby my home, was something I often did during the morning. Today, the people along the trail were friendlier than usual. An overgrown path that I was familiar with lead me a short distance to the solitude that I was seeking. I sat down on a log beside a pond that is replenished by clear running water. Standing in front of me were tall dead trees which had the appearance of weathered old totem poles. Chickadees frolicked around me in the beautiful golden leaf trees, chirping away. Closing my eyes, I felt a oneness with nature. It's like living in the present moment, when all of life's hardships are temporarily lifted. Opening my eyes, I felt refreshed, with a new outlook on life, I went peacefully along the rest of the day.

Dec 6, 1989

A spiritual experience tonight on the trail. Tonight was cool and clear as I rode my bike along my favorite bending trail. I was bundled up in gloves and a toque. I passed the odd person. I stopped along the trail and sat on my bike to rest; the moon beamed onto me and the surrounding trees. I rested my eyes for awhile and experienced the quietness. Going into a meditative consciousness, my deceased friends came to mind. Coming out of meditation, I gently opened my eyes. The white trunk poplar trees surrounding me, gleamed like a bright light. A strong radiant presence of my deceased friends seemed to surface from the poplar trees around me, entering me with incredible joy and peace. Closing my eyes again, I imagined that I was one of these trees. It was like being the branch, and the roots of the tree were God, causing me to feel very much uplifted inside. In my heart, I do believe it was a spiritual sign. God was showing me, that he is in full control of everything. And that I am part of the linkage, that he loves unconditionally. I am learning that, to know God more, I have to be in a quiet atmosphere and meditate on him, and listen to his message he is sending out.

March 31, 1990
Tonight my mind is dazed, confused and restless. My goals in life seem to be a procrastination. Distractions and the reality of life just get in the way. Everything inside me is cluttered, my dreams are at a distance tonight, I feel drained. The atmosphere and surroundings that I live around is not healthy. Feelings of loneliness creep deep within me. But I hope for a better day tomorrow.

April 7, 1990 Easter Time
Today I surrendered to God, and let him come into my heart and show me his way. Tears flowed down my cheeks like they never have before. I felt refreshed afterwards. Thinking of Jesus being crucified, I felt his presence, and tried to share some of his suffering that he went through.

May 30, 1990
While out walking tonight I decided to take a stroll past where I grew up till I was a teeny bopper. Things sure have changed. I stood and gazed at our old home for awhile, then I walked to the

corner, stood in the dark and breathed in the air. Reminiscing about my childhood days, I am interrupted by a car which travels quickly by me. A young couple walk by, I say hello, but no response. Their behavior does not bother me, I am content. Deciding to leave now, I walk the 2 miles back home in the quiet night. My childhood days may be behind me forever, but God will always be there for me.

June 24, 1990 Sunday
John the Baptist's birthday today. This sentence is a quote out of my church's weekly bulletin today. In the moments that seem the darkest, we are often most glorified.

June 26, 1990 The Spider
I am looking out the window of an unoccupied shack to the ocean.
The weary ones rest
while the energetic go all day
Their webs they test
Some dangle in a beautiful way
For I am their guest
At Qualicum Bay.

Life
Life is like a quick spin.
Where many think you are here to win.
Even if it means walking over your own kin.
It's too bad Adam and Eve ever sinned.

W.J. McKay

June 27, 1990
My wise grandmother once told me her theory of purgatory. The burning feeling of one's mind.

July 10, 1990
Today a nice lady emerged from an old blue van and gave me her bus day pass. I believe if you help and treat people the way that you would like to be treated, you are always rewarded when you least expect it (and usually it is when you need it the most.)

July 12, 1990
This quote is from God's minute book that I have in my collection. "Our father, help us to find the secret of the Master's joy, that we may no longer dwell in the outer courts where our happiness comes and goes as the flowers bloom and fade."

This other quote is from out of a pamphlet that I read: "Do not be ashamed poor soul; there are in heaven so many saints who had these same defects; but they prayed humbly and little by little they saw themselves freed from them." This quote is talking about being angry, loving pleasure, being proud, variable, negligent . . . God is saying, just ask and he will free you from these faults.

My Grandmothers Wisdom (Patricia G. O'Malley)

Each generation develops its own slang and witticism according to its surrounding circumstances or history. Contemporary beings understand these things, but as a new generation appears, often the expressions of the former generation are not meaningful – their jokes etc. – and since youth is in a hurry, they often lose contact with older people. As time passes, a person's whole being slows down. It's harder to keep up with the speed of young people's conversation as hearing dulls. The elderly often miss part of the conversation or become frustrated and abandon the effort. So often their lack of interest is thought of as aging or senility by other people. When dealing or visiting older people, one must always remember to think that some day one may reach the same state (toleration). It will develop patience.

July 24, 1990
It is very easy, I contemplated today, to get caught up in the hustle bustle of life. Treat yourself, take thirty minutes (at least?) out of your day for your own pleasure. And never take things for granted. Live life to its fullest, after all we are only here for a short period of time.

July 25, 1990
This quote came from an old apostleship of prayer leaflet: "Your weakness and your falls - when God allows them - should not separate you from Christ, but rather draw you closer to him."

July 30, 1990
Presently, for the summer, I am working as a security guard for a yacht club. Well, a club member came into the boat office tonight to pick up his key. We chit chatted for awhile. His last words of advice to me that warm muggy night,

have haunted me to this day. He reminded me that I was one day closer to death, so enjoy the sunny day and not take it for granted.

August 9, 1990
In the midst of the confusion and stress around me, I feel the need of you today God. You are a necessity to us all. Without you we cannot live, and without you we dare not die. Our spirits cannot rest until they rest in you.

Sept 6, 1990
Human behavior has caused me grief and wondering this past week. When I procrastinate and do not settle my disputes, my mind is in an unbalanced state. I feel that an acquaintance has done that to me. While sitting I gaze at the telephone on the table. Should I call or not? Meanwhile, next door, a house is being built. The noise is unbearable. There is loud music, the sound of driving nails, and unnecessary yelling, enough to make anyone crazy. I wish I could toss this heavy burden, that I am carrying, out into the sea. Most of the time I will give credit to someone that I have gotten to know. But maybe sometimes it's better to

follow your own intuition, and give your dog a big hug. Momentarily the negative atmosphere of noise next door is pounding in my head. The timing, to phone my friend and sort matters out, is not right. So I will procrastinate once again.

Sept 11, 1990
This afternoon I became annoyed with all the racket next door. (They are building next door.) I decided to leave my house and go to the library nearby. I picked up a religious magazine and thumbed through the table of contents. I came across an article of interest and began to read it. It started to say that "Christ said every trial must be borne for the sake of eternal life. My promise of eternal life will strengthen and console you. You will not labor here long. What you do, do well. Write, read, sing, mourn, keep silence, pray and bear hardships like a mother. Eternal life is worth all these and greater battles. Peace will come on a day which is known to the lord. Then there shall be no day or night as at present, but perpetual light, infinite brightness, lasting peace, and safe repose. If you could see the everlasting crowns of the saints in heaven, and the great glory where in

they now rejoice - you would certainly humble yourself at once to the very earth. Nor would you desire the pleasant days of this life, but rather be glad to suffer for God, considering it your greatest gain to be counted as nothing among men." Well this above summary of what Jesus points out to us is very true, today and everyday of our lives. So pilgrim keep persevering onwards.

Sept 29, 1990
These paragraphs are quotations from the book of, The Imitation of Christ. Chapter 31 "People are concerned to know the greatness of a man's achievements; they are not so interested in assessing the underlying goodness of his life. Is he brave, wealthy, good looking? Is he a good writer, a good singer, a good worker? These are the questions they ask. He may be humble, patient, gentle, and live a devout inner life, but you won't get many people to mention any of that. Nature looks at a man from the outside; Grace turns its gaze inward. Nature often makes mistakes; Grace trusts in God, fearing to be deceived." Chapter 43 "I am he who in a moment can so lift up the mind

of a humble man that he has a firmer grasp of the ways of external truth than the man who has spent ten years studying the subject at a university."

Oct 15, 1990
Off and on for two days, I had experienced a dark period, struggling with the fear of paranoia. I was with my mother on both occasions, in Reno, Nevada on a vacation. She was upset to see me that way, but there was not much I could do but pray that the evil one would flee and leave me at peace. I can never recall ever going through such a dark period in my life. My grandmother said some saints went through what I experienced. To hear my grandmother talk about the lives of such men served to elevate and strengthen my character. Reading the lives of the saints will awaken religious sentiments in our souls, and will teach us that they possessed peace and happiness, even when they endured the hardest trials and suffered most. They excel in the virtues of humility and courage. They allow no obstacle to stand in the way of that service.

My father, USA Navy, about 23 years old.

Gerry O'Malley's Wedding, April 14, 1956.
(Also Mommy Pat's Birthday (Gerry's Mother).
Mother's five sisters and six brothers.

Ellen O'Malley (aunt), Bill McKay, Gerry McKay. Easter Sunday, Cut Bank, Montana, June 1957. (They made their own easter outfits.)

My grandmother, (Patricia G. O'Malley), my father, mother, and myself, July, 1957.

My mother and myself at seven months of age, 1957.

My father and myself, 1958.

Bill and Michael McKay with Lucky, the dog, Summer 1960.

My father, younger brother and myself with Lucky (the dog), 1960.

Father and Mother, summer 1960.

Easter 1963.

Mother and Father at the Candlelight Ball, 1964. Held at Hotel Vancouver (Sacred Heart Convent Dance - Mother's school).

Mother and Father, Candlelight Ball, 1964.

Mother and Father, 1964.

In 1996 I was looking through some old photographs.
One particular photo caught my eye, I noticed an
apparition right above my cousins head. (My brothers
and sisters and some of my cousins are pictured
here.) The more I looked at it, the more I thought it
was my departed father. Very excited with my find, I
decided that I would get this area of the picture
enlarged. A few days later my photograph was
enlarged, and I had this feeling it was the apparition
of my father. (My father died of a brain aneurysm on
Sept 4, 1966. He was forty five years old.) My
youngest sister who is standing in the playpen, was

celebrating her first birthday, July 25, 1967, in the backyard of our home. As I studied this enlargement, I began to think that my father wanted to be present at my sister's first birthday. If you look closely, it seems that my father is looking in the direction of my sister in the playpen. I believe that telepathy was happening with the children outside the playpen, that were facing my father's apparition. And it also played a part with my sister in the playpen, my cousin in the playpen, and my sister standing outside of the playpen. That same day I looked through various photo's of my father, from the time he was young and up until the day that he died. Then I got the idea, that I would make a collage of my father. This was done by using photo copied photographs of my father. Then I would cut and glue his face on a photo copied apparition sheet of paper. The following two pages is my conception of heaven where my father is finally at home, but always watching over his loved ones.

Mother and brothers and sisters at grandmother's, 1967.

*Four years after
Dad died, 1970.*

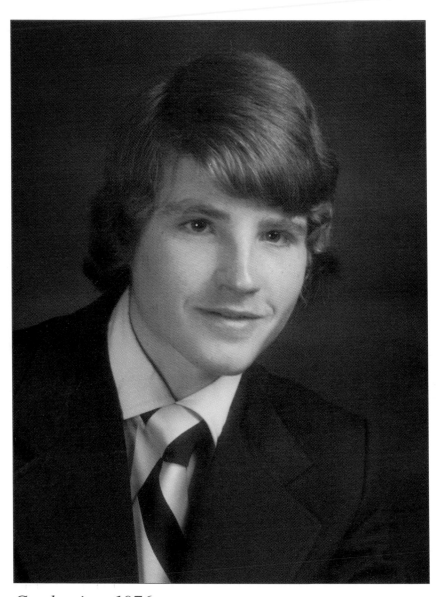

Graduation, 1976.

The following art work is done by the author.

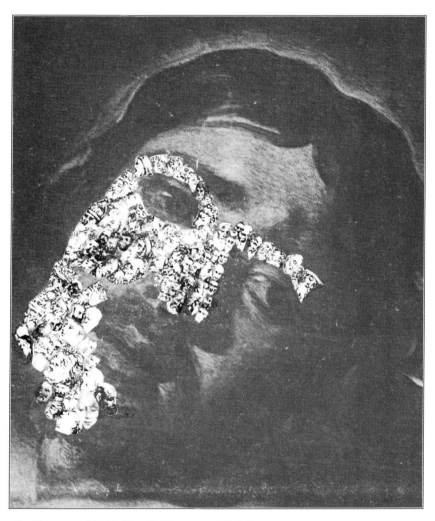

Collage of Biblical Faces, 1990.

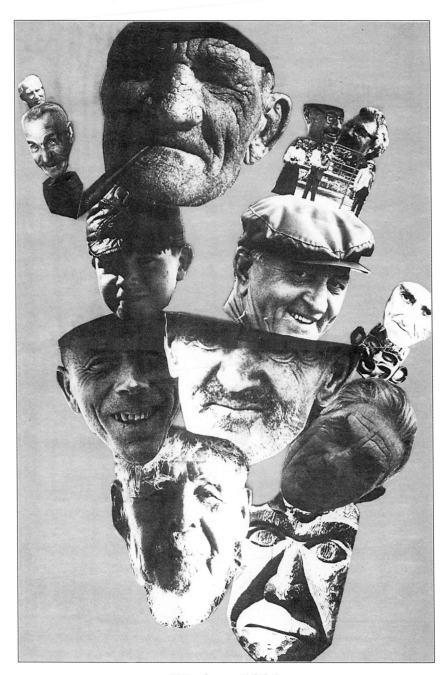

Wisdom, 1991.

Photocopy of painting my deceased aunt did back in 1960's.

Experimenting with tangled coloured thread on a photo copier machine, 1992.

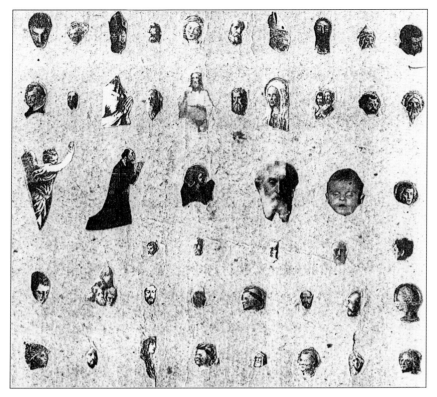

Collage of Biblical Faces, 1993

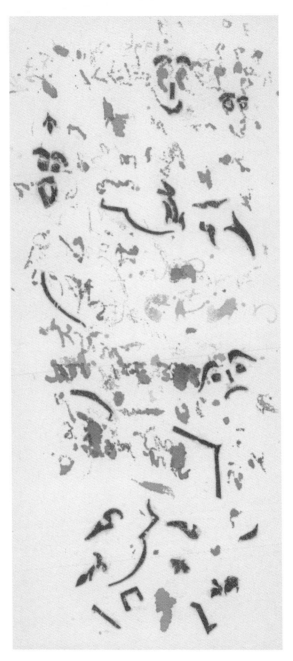

Ink blotter and collage combined to illustrate a totem pole, 1995.

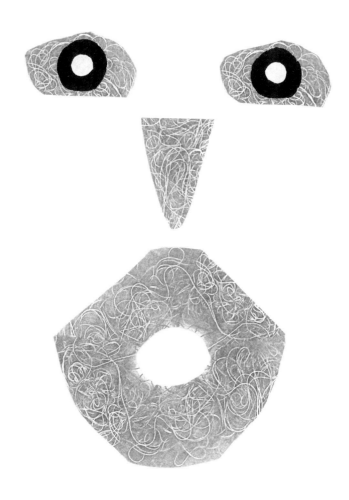

Collage of mask done with photo copied tangled thread, 1996.

Winter scene using pastel, 1997.

My method of a totem pole done in collage form, 1997.

Virgin Mary, carved from a piece of found driftwood, 1998.

Jesus, carved from a piece of found driftwood, 1998.

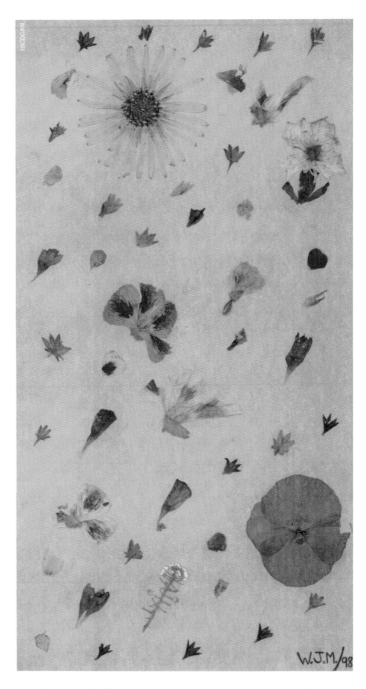

Pressed flowers pasted on paper, 1998.

"Bill" – done by Barry Mckay (the author's brother), 1998, Vancouver, BC Canada.

HEAVEN

Angels of flight, take to the flickering skies of the light,
divine and beautiful of sheer elegance of delight, deities
destined.

We dare not question, everything is connected, as we are
affected.

As footsteps of the unpaved are made down the years, they
slowly begin to fade, apparitions of one's thought ghostly
visions once taught, pulling down the years of the past
decades coming fast.

The older that we see doesn't mean the older will be.

Arms open wide, minds begin to glide, splendour and beauty
coincide, higher and higher we fly putting ourselves in
overdrive.

Freedom to roam, discovering our new home.

Everything is one, everything is fun, flying high over the
solar sun.

Minds wide, minds abide, telepathic messages worldwide.

From heaven and earth we give you this verse.

We are the guardians of the universe.

Dreamscape

Barry McKay
02/02/96

Airals of time, Pass through my mind, Pulling me through to an astral Blue, orange and red, shimmering through my head, lying comfortably here on my bed, sparkles of starlight glisten, as my mind begins to listen, opening up the portholes of my brain, everything in my room begins to drain, pulling me through to a different plane, time is one, time is none, flying high over the solar sun, luminous balls of fire, stare at me with desire, mind begins to melt, flying through an asteroid belt, like a superman on speed, the faster I go the more I need, time begins to warp, time begins to bend, hurdling me through to where there's no end, hitting ten times the speed of light, I'm no where to be seen, no where in sight, thunder claps are heard, feeling free as a bird, portholes of my mind, begin to unwind, pulling me back in through time, falling like shooting stars, just passing over the top of Mars, earth becoming distant, will be there in a split second instant, waking in my bed, feeling's of a throbbing in my head, as I'm looking around my room, I look through my window, and I see the moon, at that instant, I saw in the distance, a flickering light, flying bright, heading north into the night, like my dream, I thought it was all so sorren, asking myself, what it all really means, as though then, and only then, realizing, its where our spirits fly, once seen.

"Bill" Figure Line Design
by Celeste Red Feather
C98 Vancouver, B.C. Canada.

My great, great uncle, who has been an inspiration in my life (Rev. Stephen Eckert, O.M. CAP.,).

Rev. Stephen Eckert, O.M. Cap.,

Father Stephen Eckert was born at Dublin, Ontario, Canada, April 28th, 1869. He pursued his classical studies at Berlin (now Kitchener), Canada. On May 21st, 1891, he entered the Capuchin Order at Detroit, Mich. He was ordained a priest of God, July 2nd, 1896.

For many years New York was the field of his priestly activity. He was highly esteemed as a zealous missionary and a capable retreat-master. Neither the glamour of the metropolis nor the regard he merited therein were to his liking. Father Stephen longed to serve the poor and the neglected. Finally yielding to his petitions the superiors appointed him to St. Benedict's Mission for the black People at Milwaukee, Wisconsin. Here the zealous missionary found his life's work and – his death.

His robust physical strength, his ready gift of speech, his optimistic enthusiasm and his unbounded trust in divine Providence were henceforth made to serve the one sole purpose of his life – to uplift the black people. For this he laboured among the blacks themselves and among the whites. He was the loving father, and the valiant champion of a downtrodden race. He used every available opportunity of removing prejudice and of establishing understanding for and sympathy with the black man. Thus he traversed the state of Wisconsin and the Middle West and it was on one of these tours that he contracted the disease (pneumonia) which proved fatal. On February 16th, 1923, he breathed his last. "Here I lie idle while thousands of souls are perishing!" was one of the last utterances that escaped his fever parched lips. Since then numerous favours, spiritual and temporal, have been attributed to his intercession.

· · ·

Oct 25, 1990
Men would choose to be poor, in order to be free.

Oct 27, 1990
These paragraphs are from God's Minute Book.
"May our experience of earthly love bring us
nearer to thy love, O Thou lover of our souls!"
"When the duties of the day are done, may it
please thee to gather us at eventide an unbroken,
happy family, with no stain of sin upon our
garments."

Nov 27, 1990
From God's Minute Book. "May every day make
thee more real to us, until at last no other friend
shall be so near." (Becoming closer to God, day by
day.)

April 11, 1991
Sitting in my kitchen this morning I was looking
through the open doorway into my bedroom. Up
on one of my shelves there is a beautiful picture
called 'The Presence'. (A copy of a painting done
in a cathedral.) What caught my eye was the
illumination that the artist painted in the picture.

Beaming horizontal down the middle of the Cathedral to the front alter, it enlightened me. It then became clear to me in thought that many times in my life I have veered off the straight path. For example it is like starting at the back pew of the church, and working your way gradually up each bench individually, until at last you reach the blessed sacrament on the altar. There is where God waits ever so patiently to be at unity with you in life's trials. When you surrender to God, he will give you the grace to perform your daily duties. Through this positive move you are slowly purifying your soul before God. These are the above thoughts that came easily to my mind that morning, as I gazed in wonder at the picture called 'The Presence'.

April 15, 1991 Jericho Surroundings

As I sat up against a log, sitting on the ground, I looked up between the branches of a tree, where the moon was heavenly bound. Straight in front of me, on top of a small evergreen tree, a large owl suddenly landed . And all around me were these brown, black, white, and different sized rabbits on the prowl. For it was a beautiful spring night. And in the quietness, I could hear the sound of many frogs. Looking to the east I could see the city lights.

May 2, 1991

Thank you Lord, for sending me daily, on the path that winds, where souls may be glad that I traveled their way. With every little God given experience, my faith, hope and love in God and the people that I meet, slowly increases.

May 7, 1991

"Strengthen us that we may shun every allurement of sin, and grow daily in the knowledge and love of our savior, so that when we nightly pitch our moving tents, we may be a days march nearer home. We ask it in the name of Jesus. Amen." (Out of God's minute book.)

May 9, 1991

"That out of sorrow and suffering, we may gain strength and patience." (Out of God's minute book.)

July 10, 1991
Our father, help us to find the secret of the master's joy, that we may no longer dwell in the outer courts, where our happiness comes and goes, as the flowers bloom and fade.

Nov 29, 1991
If I could only see the light, then there would be no more darkness, no more night. Just like a blind man I wandered along today, worries and fears I kept from my own.

Jan 8, 1992 Prayer in Distress Psalm 38
Yahweh, do not punish me, in your rage your arrows have pierced deep. Your hand has pressed down on me. No health in my bones, because of my sin. My wounds stink and are festering.

April 17, 1992 Good Friday
Teach us how greatly to live and greatly to love Lord, and at the evening time of life may there be light. Amen.

Oct 7, 1992
God's idea for your life is a peaceful idea. He is

not the author of confusion. Always, our God will be interested in what we are, rather than what we did.

Oct 29, 1992

It's so easy to give in to the feeling that you are not worth anything anymore. Jesus said, "Men ought always to pray, and not to give up." (Luke 18:1) But prayer still changes people and people change things. You can confidently pray and call on Jesus in your desperate need, you will discover you have a new option! The option of trying again and seeing your dreams come true after they have seemed shattered forever. You can have the spirit of God flowing in your life.

Nov 3, 1992
Don't worry, everything does work out

Anxiety overpowered my reflection this morning. The whole of my world was behind double doors and I wasn't even thinking about faith, or trust, or anything else so "spiritual". I feared. I was about to lose my life. My world was collapsing, and in a moment I hurled myself upon God's mercy. Actually, that was probably the greatest act of faith in my entire life! For in that moment of abandon, I allowed God to do the one thing I needed more than all else - to give me his peace! Almost moments after I prayed, it happened. It was as though God, for the moment, anesthetized all my emotions. I felt entirely calm and at ease. Deep down inside I was at rest. Somehow I knew inner quiet and certitude. It was during this time that I began to comprehend just what God had done for me.

Nov 10, 1992
A friend and myself listened to some mellow music this evening. What she said during our rendezvous touched my heart. "She could not help, but think of all the sadness in the world."

Nov 17, 1992 Corinthians 10:31
God is not concerned about where you live or what you do for a living as he is about what you are. Paul wrote "Whether you eat or drink or whatever you do, do all to the glory of God."

Nov 28, 1992
Our Father, who art in Heaven, defend us in the time of temptation, and help us to realize that we

are citizens of the spiritual kingdom. Bless all our fellow disciples the world around.

Feb 8, 1993

Staring into my mirror this morning, I realized how time is slipping away forever. And deep down inside, I feel positive, and ready to venture out into a new day.

March 23, 1993

Christ's redeeming love is not restricted. He is the saviour of the world, all peoples, all races, all colors. In the words of St. Paul to the Romans: "For there is no distinction between Jew and Greek; the same Lord is Lord of all and bestows his riches upon all who call upon Him." (10:12)

April 4, 1993

"There is no better or more necessary work than love." Words from Saint John of the Cross. His feast day is Dec 14.

May 9, 1993

I met a man named Frank today; he said to me that God gave him the freedom to live a modest life.

He does not want to live up to the world, like everybody else does.

May 15, 1993
From the book of The Imitation of Christ
"Draw my senses toward you Lord and make me forget all worldly things."

May 16, 1993
From the God's minute book Pg. 131
Help me Lord to put down that desire I so frequently find taking possession of me, to make exploration here and there, beyond the boundaries you have marked off, and to be content to follow you in paths that are safe.

May 25, 1993
When people understand each other, they don't have to look up each other's actions in the dictionary, to fathom meanings.

June 17, 1993
I was being selfish at the time, and all day long my consciousness alerted me of what was right. We will be judged someday, by how much love we gave on earth.

June 24, 1993

God has shown me his infinite love over and over, in the many different situations of my life, by sending beautiful people my way to love, care, and talk to.

June 25, 1993

I phone my mother tonight to chat, she said she was thinking of me as I was dialing her telephone number. Mental telepathy I guess, because we are close.

July 2, 1993

Crossed paths with an old friend today. I asked him how he was doing, he replied that there is a battle going on with the spirit and soul, and he feels stressed, because of it. He also said, that I am a fortunate man.

July 30, 1993

Talked with a wise native woman outside Dairy Queen today. She was from Nova Scotia, Canada, going to school in Vancouver, B.C. She thanked me for talking with her. She told me, if you want to get anything accomplished in this life, that you have to gnaw at it, until it is done.

Oct 15, 1993
Watched an adventure show on television tonight. Lord Jim was the name of it. One of the sayings they used in the show was, that Lord Jim <u>jumped into the unknown</u>. This underlined phrase reminds me of myself, when I have in the past, gone on adventurous trips not knowing what to expect.

Oct 26, 1993 Fall
It is now fall,
and the trees around me stand tall,
The wind blows and the leaves go astray,
Landing on the ground, in a beautiful array.
William J. McKay

Nov 9, 1993 The Radiant Personality
There is something depressing about the sight of a house with the shades all drawn. I want to get by it as soon as possible. And that's the way I feel about many human beings that I meet or pass - their shades are all drawn. Life is away!

Nov 14, 1993

The topic of the sermon at church today was our talents as individuals. The sermon reminded us that God is the God of surprises, who encourages us to take a dangerous chance and dare, rather than bury our power of body, mind, position etc. If we live with a deep trust in God, we have the freedom to try the new and different knowing, that he is with us whether we succeed or fail.

Jan 12, 1994

A genuine friend, that I had coffee with this morning, made an excellent point that impaled me. "We were brought up in a time when things were strict. So if we were adventurous when we were young, by the time we are older, we would have lost the way of being adventurous."

Feb 3, 1994 Feeling Blue

Strolling the ocean shoreline today, I picture the thought of growing older. And as I get older society seems to becoming colder. Momentarily I am distracted, by a low flying blue heron. But soon it's gone, and I am back to thinking, of how humans can be so barren.

William J. McKay

March 14, 1994
"What Work Is" by Philip Levine
What work is, you love your brother, now
suddenly you can hardly stand the love flooding
you for your brother, who's not beside you or
behind or ahead but is elsewhere. How long has it
been since you told him you loved him, held his
wide shoulders, opened your eyes wide and said
those words, and maybe kissed his cheek?

March 21, 1994
The secret to beauty is a clean soul.

March 23, 1994
by Father Tabe - March 23, 1922
My life is but a weaving
Between my God and me;
I may but choose the colors -
He worketh steadily.
Fulloft He weaveth sorrow,
And I, in foolish pride,
Forget He sees the upper
And I the under side.

April 21, 1994 Psalm 32:3-4
David described the discipline of the Lord this
way: "When I kept silent about my sin, my body
wasted away through my groaning all day long.
For day and night thy hand was heavy upon me;
My vitality was drained away as with the fever -
heat of summer."

April 26, 1994
Throughout my life, I have walked many circles.
Always trying to wait patiently for the right time,
to make the right decision.

Nov 14, 1994
Do not worry about tomorrow, today has enough
to do in itself.

Jan 23, 24 & 25, 1995
I had not seen an old school friend for twenty
years, and then I encountered him on three
different occasions. He made a joke out of it and
said, "We have to stop meeting like this."

Jan 28, 1995 Are You Lonesome
Could a person be lonesome -

Could a woman be blue -
If ever you feel lonesome or
If ever you feel blue -
Just come to me and I will try
to make you feel like you -
I'll hug you and I'll love you,
And I will make you smile,
I'll tell you such a funny tale,
and pet you all the while.

Free
In my life,
I do not have a wife,
It does have its advantages,
Where I can unravel all my bandages.
Like being on an open sea,
Is where I have learned, to be me.

William J. McKay

Introspect
There's an old saying,
everything has its way.
It's either living or decaying,
today is an overcast day.
I sit on my sun deck,

and watch a bird,
feeling like a wreck,
but in my mind absurd.
It balances on last years withered bean vine
"Wailing and grinding of beak."
Understanding it, a divine sign,
inside thoughts of seethe.

William J. McKay

The Encounter

Crossed paths today with an elder,
that is what I had first thought.
His clothing was not that of a welder,
my second thought, it was naught.

But an old native friend of mine
once told me of this old heritage site.
It was behind a sturdy vine
is where he saw a radiant figure of light.

For one thousand years, his people were buried
here. Standing still, remembering his story, I
was in awe.
I could feel this elder's presence still so near,
this is no misunderstanding what I felt and saw.

The sun going down behind the autumn leaves,
with its brilliance upon the Fraser Angus lands.
And up ahead he crossed pathways, moving swiftly
wearing a former attire, with arms
outstretched with flowing sleeves.
The truth this elder already knows, the joy of
praising hands.

William J. McKay

One Legged Man

Making his way up the street, he paused for a rest,
I was walking on the opposite side.
In a hurry heading west,
he balanced on crutches, gazing at me abide.

The second time I saw him,
I was sitting at the bus stop.
He stopped and chatted about meeting Tiny Tim,
another person's opinion, he's eccentric, mine
he's the top.

He talked about his encounter with Elvis Presley
in Vancouver in nineteen fifty-nine.
He said he was gentle, and had beautiful eyes
of blue.

When he had heard of his death, he became in
   pine, his pang was to frequent his favorite
   solitary slough.
His telepathy-fixed stare I perceived as real,
   then he asked me my name, and I told him.
He then had to go, and did so with zeal,
   arms and hands clutching his crutches,
   supporting his one limb.

William J. McKay

The Logger

With the passing of time,
still stands the stumps, of the old forest tree.
Oh what a hideous crime,
Why could not the logger foresee.

William J. McKay

Summer's Night

Oh refreshing wave,
On such a muggy night.
It is you that I crave,
you are such a beautiful sight
between the bank, and the angry waves at my feet,
   I brave,
With the wind at my back, and careless as a
   straying kite.

Actively united with the holy spirit, I present my
soul, and you save..

William J. McKay

The Lesson

The wind has a meaning,
the moon has a magnetic force.
The moon beautiful beaming,
the wind blows its own random course.

We are all searching for the right profession,
We then harvest the knowledge, and we die.
We human beings, are here to learn that lesson,
We then are set apart or elected, by our almighty high..

William J. McKay

Hopeful

I am sluggish in my mind with quest,
because doing things still my way.
I often wonder about the place of the blest,
sustaining life, with the aid of my departed father,
Ray.
Oh also, how inspiring is the name celest,
but all I can hope for, is that blissful new day..

William J. McKay

Graveyard Shift - My present occupation
Position Title: Security, Night Watch Person, Front Desk Clerk. Responsible for one hundred and twenty senior residents in hi-rise building. Routine after routine. Garbage collection throughout the buildings nineteen floors. Setting up tables and chairs in recreational room for next day's schedule. Responsible for residents' daily newspaper distribution. Vacuuming first floor. Polishing pictures and windows. Fighting drowsiness, beginning to get cranky. Sometimes I listen to Art Bell on fourteen C-Fun. All my work is usually finished by 7:30 AM. Between 7:30 AM and 7:55 AM, the day staff start to arrive. Same questions: How was your night? I reply it was quiet, their reply: That's good to hear. Just around the corner from where I work I catch the 8:10 AM UBC express bus home. Most of the time I stand, holding the rail on the bus, because the seats are all occupied. Periodically I close my eyes and grasp the rail tightly. When I reach home, I sometimes visit my neighborhood MacDonald's, and order their big breakfast. Halfway through my breakfast I am usually cranky like a bear. When I arrive home I feel obligated to floss and brush my teeth before

sleeping, because I have been sucking on Purdy's chocolates at work to stay awake. Finally I open my window for air, set my alarm, crawl into bed, and hope that I hear my alarm go off.

Published Poetry

1. Primal St James Community Square 3214 West 10th Avenue Vancouver, B.C. Canada V6K 2L2. Published in August 1995 *Illusion*.
2. The National Library of Poetry, 1 Poetry Plaza Owings Mills, Maryland 21117-6282. Published in 1997 anthology *A Treasured Token*.
3. Rideau Manor 1850 Rosser Avenue Burnaby, B.C. Canada, V5C 5E1. Published in April 1997 *Curtain Call*, a monthly newsletter.
4. The Amherst Society published, in 1997 *American Poetry Annual*.
5. Poets Guild published in 1997 anthology *Best New Poems*.
6. The Poetry Guild, 3687 Ira Road P.O. Box 5010 Bath, Ohio, published in 1997 anthology *Idyllic Thoughts*.
7. Iliad Press 36915 Ryan Road Suite 1 Sterling Heights, Michigan 48310 Published in 1997 edition *Treasures* their 27th literary hardcover anthology.
8. American Poetry Guild, INC. Box 438, Riderwood, MD 21139-0438. Published in 1997 anthology.

9. Quill Books P.O. Box 3109 Harlingen, TX 78551
10. Sparrowgrass Poetry Forum, 609 Main St. P.O. Box 193. Sistersville, WV 26175. (Published in the spring 1998 edition of *Poetic Voices of America*, a national hardcover anthology.)
11. JMW Publishing Company, Blue Springs, MO 64013 Published in 1998 annual anthology, *Visions.*
12. Creative Arts and Scient ENT. 341 Miller Street Abilene, TX 79605 published in 1998 anthology.

If you want to write me, my address is
563 West 23rd Avenue
Vancouver, B.C.
Canada V5Z 2A4